I
is for
ISRAEL

Written by **Gili Bar-Hillel**

Photographs by **Prodeepta Das**

Frances Lincoln
Children's Books

Many people feel very strongly about Israel, even if they don't live here but feel connected to the land because of their family, religion or nationality.

You might hear news about Israel that sounds frightening: war, conflict and struggles. And yet people lead normal daily lives here. We have our joys, our loves and our celebrations. There is always a yearning for a better life, for justice, for peace.

I hope this book will show you a little bit of the good side of life in Israel, and what we can all enjoy, whatever our beliefs or backgrounds. Perhaps the children of today can build upon these things we all love, to reach understanding in the future, and live in peace.

Gili Bar-Hillel

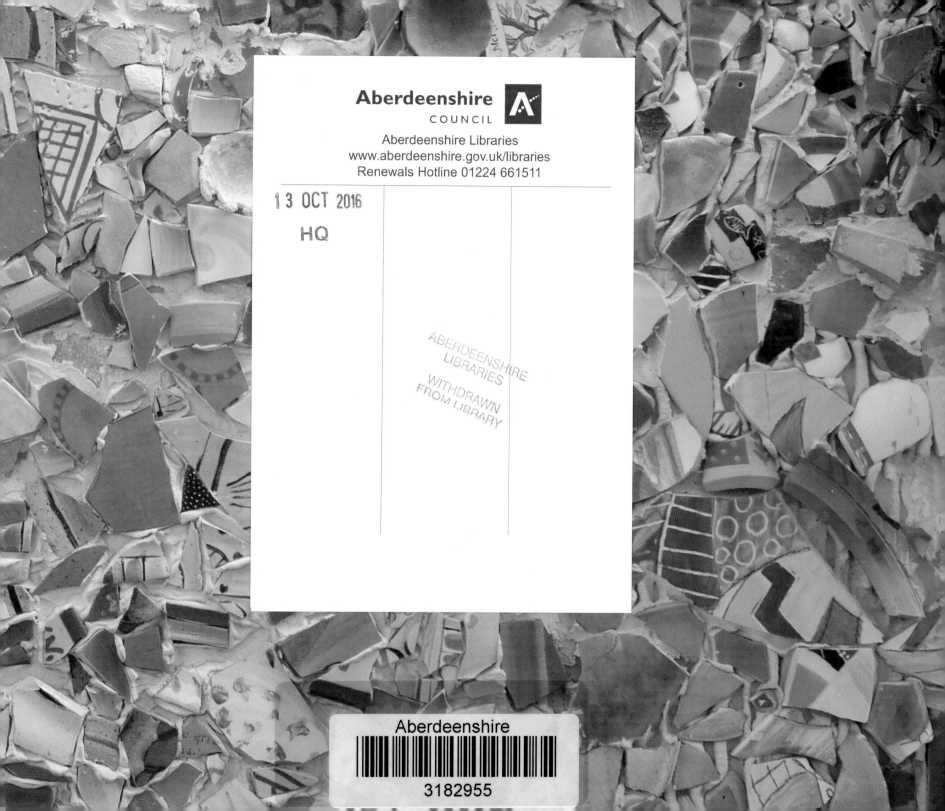

Heartfelt thanks to Victor Priel and the Peretz family of Kibbutz Revivim, to Shoshana Dan of
The Ben-Gurion National Solar Energy Center, to the students and staff of Ulpan Degania-Neve Zedek,
to the pupils and teachers of Gavrieli-HaCarmel Elementary School, and most of all to my amazing,
generous and supportive husband, Hemi: life would be impossible without you. — GBH

A huge thank you to Janetta for commissioning me to photograph a fascinating country,
Hemi for his friendship and guidance and Abraham Tours for hospitality — PD

JANETTA OTTER-BARRY BOOKS

Text copyright © Gili Bar-Hillel 2016
Photographs copyright © Prodeepta Das 2016
The rights of Gili Bar-Hillel and Prodeepta Das to be identified as the author and photographer of this work
have been asserted by them in accordance with the Copyright, Designs and Patents Act, 1988 (United Kingdom).

First published in Great Britain and in the USA in 2016 by
Frances Lincoln Children's Books,
74-77 White Lion Street, London, N1 9PF
QuartoKnows.com
Visit our blogs at QuartoKnows.com

A CIP catalogue record for this book is available from the British Library.

ISBN 978-1-84780-708-3

Set in Granjon and Cabin

Printed in China

9 8 7 6 5 4 3 2 1

 A is for
Ahalan!
Shalom! Hello,
and welcome!

Ahalan is short for *Ahalan waSahalan* in Arabic, a welcome greeting. Most people in Israel speak Hebrew, but many speak Arabic, and each language borrows from the other. So don't be surprised if Israelis greet you with a big smile and a warm, drawn-out "Ahalaaaan!"

B is for Birds

Each year, wild cranes like these, and other birds migrating between Africa and Europe, fly through the skies of Israel. About half a billion birds visit Israel in this way, including more than 490 different species. At the Hula Nature Reserve in northern Israel, the birds are provided with grain to eat, to discourage them from raiding farms and fields.

C is for Caesaria

Caesaria is an ancient port city that has fallen and been rebuilt again and again over the centuries. Ancient Greeks, Romans, Byzantines, Muslims, Crusaders and Ottomans built their temples and strongholds here, each on the ruins of the other. Some of the ancient ruins have crumbled into the sea and can be seen under the waves.

D is for
Dead Sea

This sea is the lowest point on Earth, almost 430 metres below sea level. The water of the Dead Sea is so full of salts and minerals that nothing can live in it. The water feels oily when you touch it, and people float easily on its surface. Dark mud from the Dead Sea is supposed to be good for your skin – so visitors smear it all over themselves!

E is for Energy

Sunshine is plentiful in Israel, and we try to harness the energy of the sun in different ways. Most homes in Israel have solar panels to heat water; almost 8% of Israel's energy comes from solar panels. It's a good start, but we believe we have only just begun to make use of solar energy.

F is for Falafel

These deep fried balls of ground chickpeas are served in a pita bread pocket with salad, hummus and tahina. Israel is a food-lover's paradise. Immigrants from all over the world brought their favourite foods here. Some common street foods include *mlawach* and *jakhnun* from Yemen, *bourekas* from the Balkans and *couscous* from North Africa. But king of the street foods is still falafel. Watch you don't drip tahina when you try it!

G is for Gardens

The Baháʼí Gardens were planted by followers of the Baháʼí faith in the city of Haifa. They are constructed like a staircase climbing up the slope of Mount Carmel, almost a full kilometre (half a mile) in length. It is hard work keeping the gardens tended and watered, but they are a beautiful and important part of the city of Haifa.

H is for Hebrew

Hebrew is the main language spoken in Israel. The Bible was written in Hebrew, thousands of years ago. For centuries, the language was preserved by Jews, who prayed, read sacred texts and studied in Hebrew. In the 19th century, it was revived as a modern, spoken language. New words had to be invented for things like electricity, automobiles, ice-cream and tomatoes!

I is for
Israel

Israel is the only Jewish state. The area of Israel is a land bridge connecting Asia and Europe to Africa. Humans first settled here thousands of years ago, and history is all around. Today Israel is a thriving modern country, known for technological innovation.

J is for
Jerusalem

Jerusalem is the capital of the modern state of Israel, located in the Judaean Mountains. People have lived in Jerusalem for over six thousand years, and it is known as the Holy City because it is sacred to Jews, Christians and Muslims alike. According to the ancient Jewish sages, "ten measures of beauty fell upon the world: nine were given to Jerusalem, and one to the rest of the world."

K is for Kibbutz

A kibbutz is a communal way of living that is special to Israel. On a kibbutz, everything belongs to the people who live there. The income raised by members of the kibbutz is divided among all of them. In the past even the children were raised together in a "children's house", but today on most *kibbutzim* children live with their own parents.

L is for Lions

Hundreds of years ago, lions lived in this region. Lions are the symbol of the tribe of Judaea and of the city of Jerusalem. Their images can be found all over Jerusalem, from the Lions' Gate in the old city to the manhole covers on the road! We especially love these lions in the Lion Fountain, sculpted by Gernot Rumpf.

M
is for
Matkot

Matkot are the paddles used in a game of beach paddle-ball. TOK! TOK! TOK! If you walk on one of our many beaches, sooner or later you are likely to hear the unmistakable sound of a little black rubber ball bouncing off the *matkot*. Hitting the little balls is much harder than it looks – but these kids are champions at it!

N is for **Negev**

This large desert in the south of Israel covers more than half the entire country! Here you will find the huge Ramon crater, created by massive earthquakes and millennia of erosion. In the Negev you can see sand in an amazing range of colours: white, black, pink, yellow, orange, red and even blue.

O is for Olives

With their long, silvery leaves, olive trees grow everywhere in Israel. They can live to be 200, 300 or even 400 years old, and still produce fruit. In ancient days, olive oil was vital for lighting lamps. Today we use olives and olive oil mostly for cooking. Olive branches are a symbol of peace, and they decorate the shield of Israel.

P is for Purim

Purim is the silliest, funniest Jewish holiday! On Purim we dress up in costumes: you'll see queens and clowns, lions and butterflies, characters from stories and shows, and very short doctors and policemen wearing very fake beards. Some cities organise Purim parades, but who waits to be organised? Go out to the streets and party!

Q is for Qumran

The Qumran caves in the Judaean Desert are where the Dead Sea Scrolls were preserved for more than 2,000 years, until they were rediscovered in the 20th century. The scrolls serve as a link between legend and history, giving us historical evidence for events that took place in biblical times. Many families and schoolchildren visit the scrolls at the Shrine of the Book, in the Israel Museum in Jerusalem.

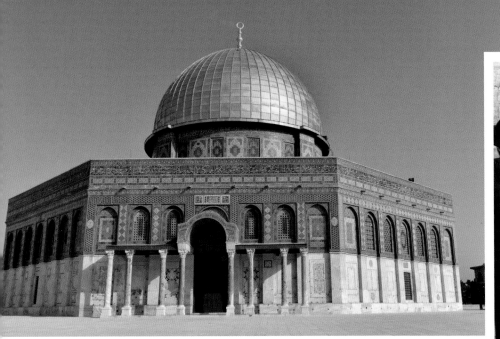

R is for Religions

Israel is known as the Holy Land because it is a place of importance to three major religions: Judaism, Christianity and Islam. For Jews this is the land of their forefathers, for Christians it is the land of Christ, and for Muslims, Jerusalem is the city from which Muhammed miraculously ascended to heaven. Many visitors to Israel are religious pilgrims who have come here because of their beliefs.

S is for **Shuk**

Going to the *shuk* – the market – is always an adventure. You can see the vivid colours of the fruit and vegetables, hear the vendors calling out in singsong, and smell the spices piled in huge sacks and bins. You may have to bargain to get the best prices, but nothing beats shopping at the *shuk*!

T is for Tel Aviv

Tel Aviv is a large, bustling city in the centre of Israel. Here, old meets new, and shiny modern high-rise buildings tower over quaint old houses with shingled roofs. Businesspeople rush from meeting to meeting, street artists leave their marks in surprising places, tourists wearing flip-flops head down to the beach and locals sit in the sidewalk cafes, watching the world go by.

U is for Ulpan

This is where new immigrants – people who come to live here, from another country – learn Hebrew. Israel is a country of immigration, that especially draws Jews from all over the world who believe this is their homeland. Learning a new language is hard for adults, and the *ulpanim* exist to make this as easy as possible.

V is for Vines

Vines are the plants on which grapes are grown. Grapes are one of the 'seven species', crops that the Bible listed as especially important to Israel. Grapes are grown all over Israel, to make into wine or just to eat off the bunch. You can even eat the vine leaves. Filled with rice or meat, and cooked, they are delicious!

W is for Water

Water is very precious in a desert land. Most of the fresh water used in Israel comes from the Kinneret lake (also known as the Sea of Galilee), but this is not enough for the needs of all the people living in Israel. So we have developed special pipes and drips for watering crops and plants in the desert. Scientists have also found ways to turn the salty sea water into usable fresh water.

 **is for**
Ibex

Ibex are mountain goats that are found mostly in the southern part of Israel, in the Negev Desert and the hills of Eilat. They trip nimbly up and down the rocky mountains. With their glorious horns, you can see why the Israeli Nature and Parks Authority chose an ibex as its symbol. You might meet ibex that seem quite tame – but please don't feed them, they are wild animals!

Y is for Yeshiva

This is a religious school for the study of Jewish law, traditions and scripture, and for orthodox (strictly religious) Jewish men, learning is a lifelong aspiration. Scholars come from all over the world to study at the *yeshivot* in cities such as Bnei Beraq, Jerusalem and Zefat.

Z is for Zionism

Zionism is the belief that the land of Israel is the historic homeland of the Jewish people. In November, 1947, Jews all over the world listened to the radio in great suspense, as the countries of the United Nations voted on whether to establish the modern state of Israel. The majority voted yes! So, in May, 1948, the first prime minister of Israel, David Ben-Gurion, declared independence right here in this very room, which you can visit as a museum today.

Gili Bar-Hillel was born in Jerusalem. She worked for
many years as a translator, and now has her own publishing
house, which publishes books for children and young adults.
She lives in Tel Aviv with her husband and three children,
a dog, a cat, two tame rats, and several thousand books.
I is for Israel is Gili's first book for Frances Lincoln Children's Books.

Prodeepta Das is an author and photographer whose
pictures have been published in over 20 children's books.
He is the photographer for many of the World Alphabet titles,
including the classic *I is for India*, which he also wrote.
His most recent book for Frances Lincoln is *A Day I
Remember – An Indian Wedding*. Prodeepta lives with his
family in east London.